PERFECT ASSERTION

S JAGATHSIMHAN NAIR

Contents

Contents

Contents

Contents

Foreword

This is my fifth collection of poems. The seventy one poems in this book are divided into two sections. The first section has just eight poems, all written based on well-known paintings. They are therefore called Ekphrastic poems. Seven of them were written for a twenty-poem-challenge run by a Canadian on-line magazine in 2015, on invitation. If I remember right, two or three of them were adjudged the best among all the entries they received and the title poem is one such. All the poems are accompanied by their respective paintings. The second section carries poems written during the years, 2018 and 2019.

1. Perfect Assertion

The unexpected beauty of imperfect things by Lorette C Luzajic

The long night of questions
also handed the morning
with a scratch card of promise.

Colors did intrude though
in an otherwise open-ended
discourse that followed.

Scouring of solid pneumonics
of colors with linear algorithms

yielded a fair surprise

leaving the domain porous
for ingress of dimensions
in a dumb co-ordinate system
gifting counter-contours
of a sing-song progress
with a singular assertion.

Inspiration: The painting " The unexpected beauty of imperfect things" by Lorette C Luzajic,2013.

2. Starry Night

Starry Night by Vincent Van Gogh

The times twist and rise like rare tornadoes
Timelines elsewhere just turn into homilies
And the stars-turned-hearts are bleeding blues
The happenstance-moon for once is not made
of light to light up our home CFL's
The rain gods do not drop water bottles
to the marooned; or the air, mantras, to reverse
Rigor mortis. The sky, hawker of visuals,
implores blind pathways to unchoke themselves.

I bide time in my twelfth floor Himalayas.
Kedar's water demons come calling,
metamorphosed into meteorology,
dunking Chennai's life in tears where float bloated
the arid wits of the metro's whirlpool gods.

Note: Inspired mainly by the VINCENT VAN GOGH painting " STARRY NIGHTS", 1889, and the Chennai(India) floods of 2015 which brought back memories of previous year's floods in Srinagar and the one in the Himalayas, the year before.

3. Raising the bar

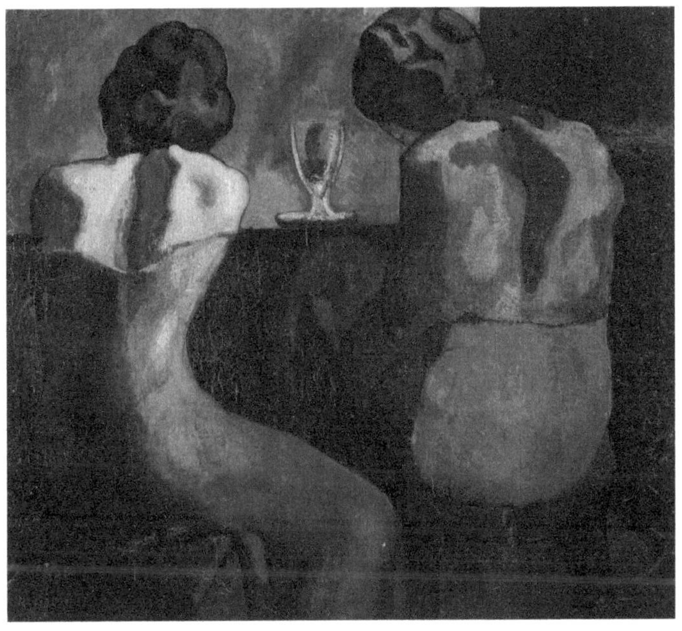

Two women sitting at a bar by Pablo Picasso

Come along, mate,
Let us cross this concourse of
coincidences and pray before this
ever-evaporating deity of oblivion.
And offer the termite hills of our doubts

at the altar of this counter-god.

Placed before his liquid justice
is our shared compendium of one mind
two heads and four arms in the form
of some kind of a binary code or joke.

Are we algebraically trying to tie up
the imponderables like
mind, head and means, or just
offering up our movables like
money and matrimony and
immovables like kids and tits.

But the new mind is a dumb platform
like meadows are just mud
And the means as always converges
to come-what-may.

Any which way, let us not go slow
into our convulsions
into contrition
into oblivion.

Inspiration: ' Two women sitting at a bar' by Pablo Picasso, 1902.
24 nov 2015.

4. The Night Cafe

The night cafe by Vincent Van Gogh

At last the clock beyond sloshed
buys into the idea of noughts.
Nought , nought, one, nought
before the open house of mathematicians.

Not this, not that,
why not, what not

Voices surged and surfed
on the network of olive green tabs
Somewhere there was an almost-ally
red and readied
not asking for a brain twister
from the o. house.

Was there a o.somebody was
the counter voice.
The keyboard knows which is o
and which is zeerroo.
The progress of the fifth pilgrim.
Time was still servicing the pace makers
The fifth column.

Dec 1, 2015.
Based on the painting 'The night cafe' by Van Gogh.

5. Virgin and Child

Virgin and Child by Sofonisba Anguissola

Matrix of allusions. Its intersections
dipped in the beckoning depths of chaste dark
to grow limbs like any other. To mark
a departure into a great mission.
Life dipped in a suave and rare medium
of strokes and streaks . Who would not sense
in the vision-flatness an equilibrium
of solidity and reassurance.

The harboring grid of hardened faith
is crowned with thorns of colored distractions
without the telling placenta of birth
but still-lifed in womb-dark meditation
I 'm the virgin, the lactating breasts, the birth
I 'm the baby of the resurgent earth.

Form: A modern Sonnet.

*Based on the painting " Virgin and child" by SOFONISBA ANGUISSOLA

26th Oct 2013.

6. The Gift of Presence

The gift of presence by Raymond Saunders

But I bear none to this confusion
flattened into a stoic time-presence .
Fine with time, may be fine too
with an engagement with variety
wherever we choose to buy peace
from purveyors of continuity.
But then, we live our days in parts
ironically linked to connectivity of sorts.
Only to be configured over time
by a cellular disengagement .
Nov 19, 2015.

Inspiration: Painting by Raymond Saunders, 'The Gift of Presence',1993

7. Dance of Lights

Dance of lights in Venice by Marek Lagowski

What is my takeaway from this
VISA card of visibility? Flashbacks from
past incarnations? Or the sun
acrobating up
A lamp post? Or dusky romance swamping
me in a swirl of blue?

Or the mappings of a modest
Receptivity stretching a pruned
moon into its full disc?
Or a report card of coherence?

Based on the painting 'The dance of lights in Venice' by Marek Lagowski

Dec 2015

8. Reading

At a Desk Reading by Frederick Leighton

Book by itself is a photon of light
Not a black hole or a blockbuster
Which is not about dark-bright stuff
But about a systematic synthesis.
It's also about memoried evenings gifting
essential takeaways and split-in-two

doubts closing up as quick-witted mornings
And the holy basil too needs to get its due.
Because its cells too need to be lit up
to grow a halo all its own.
It is but a little girl's this day.
22-11-15.
Form : Ekphrastic as part of the 20 poem challenge.

Inspiration: The painting 'At a desk reading' by Frederick Leighton, 1877.

9. Section 2

Poems of 2018 and 2019

10. 9) Beginnings

Let us now talk of the beginnings.
It is zero as usual.
Or the cold start of loadings.
Zero is nothing.
Like zilch, zombie, zip…
A dot languishing at the far end
May be as part of an ellipsis.
But is not any random letter as important.
Like say D.
Delete, dalit, delhi,,…da, da, da
Damam, daanam, daya,
in the Upanishadic order.
What wealth it carries, just a D.
Do they not cause rains to fall
and floods to flow out.
At least, do they not slow down earth.
Would they unburden life
That is never, for living, free,
Like the public toilet is,
Whenever one wants to pee.

Note: Damam : self control, Danam: Charity, Daya : compassion.

Dec 18

11. 10) St.Angelo's Fort

St Angelo's fort, Kannur.
Fortifications of the mind,
Of remembrances,
Of love,
Of even smiles, tears
All that we have seen.
Now on to a far less insidious type:
Fortifications of history
Now walked all over by every T, D, and Harry.
The virus-ridden story of these firewalls
Under the safekeeping of whatsAppers.
The moat, like conscience, has no takers.
Michelangelo, forgive me.
Dec 18

12. 11) Journey to Varanasi

Delhi looks closer than it was last time.
After an airport-tea, more GST than tea,
On to a backstreet of Varanasi,
Untouched by authority;
ignored more by memory
than darkened by amnesia.
A huge black cow lazes about,
like a Moghul monarch blocking
half the street. It won't let the OLA pass.
At the hoary-holy sanctum,
my paper cupped milk
pours on to the Lord's cosmic crown.
Ganga, here, is an old Benares
fraying at the edges, laid out to dry in the open.
So still, like *samana*, the balancing *prana*.
Human flesh fuels
the firewood at the Harichandra ghat..
Benares eyes Harichandra rather darkly.
The Ganga Arati at 6.30
The off-whiteness of it all and the huge lamps
that draw patterns in the air.
Lines with the solemn predictability
of a Ravi varma . Ganga is a new Miss World .

At the Manikarnika ghat too, bodies dutifully burn.
In the dark, death sparkles,
pampered by pundits and sanctified by Sanskrit.
I lie in an OYO at Godowlia so ill. Done in
By a glass of 'dhandai'. So close to *mukti.*
An unpretentious doctor queers my pitch..
One of a tribe long extinct in Serpent town,
his fees: 'whatever you please'.
I remember my place.
Thank god, I was not in one there.
Sure, the 'path to hell is paved
with good intentions'
(of corporates and false swamis)

Notes:

OLA : The taxi cab app, OYO : An app to find hotel rooms.

Serpent town : Trivandrum, Samana : One of the five pranas(breaths), the equalizing prana.

Nov 2018

13. 12) Burning Ghats of Varanasi

'In the beginning, there was nothing. By death was all this covered. Or by hunger. For, hunger is death indeed'.
(Brihadaranyaka Upanishad')

Huge heaps of fire gaze at me from far,
the flaming maws marking time.
I smell its smoke, holy smoke, rising;
Its classic smell, leaching through
Its lightly perfumed camouflage.
Among piles of wood stacked up like
disappointments, big and small.
Little men hover, powerless as moths.
Hungry cows circle the fires
like brides, the matrimonial fire.
Galaxies of the gods
blazing at the altars of the ghats.
One eats up ghee, the other human fate.
Upon towers of grief, the aviation lights
Pundits sit stamping away
travel papers in Sanskrit.
Not far away, gurus sell Sanskrit
to English-speaking clients.
I am blank.

No fear. No love or hate either.
What else could be in there.
Is there at least some last desire left?
And I find, of all things, hunger, in there.
But hunger is death.
Yes, death, the last in desire. That is the finding.
That is going to be the verdict too.
Mruthyuna eva idam aavrutam aseet ashnaayaya.
Death, the very first void,
Death, the hunger, with its mouth of fire
The death that gnaws at everyone's gut.
'Ashanaaya hi mruthyu'.

Notes:

Mruthyuna eva idam aavrutam aseet ashnaayaya : all this was covered by death that is hunger

Ashanaaya hi mruthyu = Hunger is death indeed.

This is from Brhadaranyaka Upanishad.

Nov 2018

14. 13) Dasara,2018, in Amritsar

Seventy Dasaras, since freedom.
Still, no Dasara-free rail tracks in Amritsar.
Celebrations like how they vote
in the elections; Freely, fearlessly.
Without looking left or right,
The moment rolling stock
Colluded with the annihilator, though.
Perhaps, busy looking
through the charter we borrowed
from the amoral west. Which, alas, carries
so much morality now;
And all our other holy ity's to boot.
Celebrating the ity's (deity excluded)
They got liberated from Dasaras.
Pity the pity-party blokes who don't.
Long live the petty party push for the 'grabs'.

Notes:

Reference is to the hundreds celebrating Dasara on the rail tracks who were run over by a train in Amritsar in Oct 2018.

Ity's : Equality, liberty etc.

Dec 2018

15. 14) ME TOO

At least in our case we were an 'us-two',
Though it had since morphed into a 'me-too'.
Like under a home loan, too heavy to bear,
I went nearly broke and yet, did not care.
But, what you did now is not that fair.
For, now, I stand to lose my home too;
Which leaves me wondering 'you too?'
20-10-18

16. 15) The Sky-seed

I thought you arose
As a huge sky
To hold those falling stars
Then I remembered father
Working his coconut grove
Who, unlike me, knew well
Stars are not trees
And sky is no earth.
Father wins the day.
Coaxed gently, you bend,
And you bend, like promises.
But by then you sneak
Into me as a seed
In stealth and grow
Not as a basil
At the holy centre
Of consensual homesteads
Not as a peepal either
With its coercive sprout
At the base of healthy walls
But as a hybrid botany of com-promises
As a bottle drained of brandy
As luv drained of love.

Sept 2018

17. 16) Moon

The train headed for the moon.
Despair was a station
where love stood in attention.
I need to be lectured
more on the need for vitamins
than on testaments.
Where did they go?
Here is the moon.
A moon a day keeps despair away.
Don't moan on a hartal day.
Dec 2018

18. 17) Keys

I lose keys in trains, in bus stations,
in arguments, even in tea cups.
The first time I lost one,
she said she had fibromyalgia.
That was how, I think, the world lost
the key to fibromyalgia.
The problem with the keys is
they always go alone.
As people in deep love do.
The deeper it is, the more alone.
And the fate of what remains
is to break in two.
As if to continue to love each other.
That is also how the world breaks.
Dec2018

19. 18) Demon's progress and democracy's demise

A prayer this is to the Lord,
From where democracy lies floored;
To shine sanitizing light
On this contaminated night.
Trashed, yes, by demons who lobbed
Questions at us at first and throbbed
With answers so prompt and pat
until, before them, we fell flat.
When they mocked at the 'old'
And it became an art that sold
And issued threats and acted smart
We applauded to our heart.
But, greed was their main creed,
Some 'ism' or the other their feed;
Movies and cricket their deities;
With those icons lay their fealties.
Their answers went awry,
They hacked up humans by and by,
Teasing grew into routine rapes
Post-rape manglings and escapes.
Mother killed son, son killed mother,
Someone else killed the 'other,

And wondered aloud if a dad
Should anymore be called a dad.
Triumphantly they marched
To where a hungry tribal reached,
Looking for a mouthful of food,
And they beat him to death, so rude.
A bun-in-the-oven woman
Then loomed in their horizon.
They kicked her belly and she bled,
Her baby-in-the-womb went dead.
This was their avowed holy rite,
The act of faith and displayed might,
Unstoppable their juggernaut,
With power centres lies their clout.
The songs of empathy they sing
Do not at all mean a thing.
It is all for the sake of form
The calm before the storm .
Democracy we have faved,
Now you want it to be saved,
And risen above poly-tricks,
Into where humanity ticks.
But, how will you save a ship
Adrift without leadership
By electing a captain from among
The random travelling throng.
5-3-18

20. 19) Green

Green, green, green
The weeping willow we have seen
On the way back from the beach,
The one hundred year old oak
The heavy hedges of beech,
The sycamores and the chestnuts
Were all green, green.
You were green
The town was green
The month was green
Even the subjective 'may's'
In the multiple may-we's of May
Until you would one day say:
But, in the coming fall
They would all lose their wigs
They would all go like twigs.
5 Apr 19

21. 20) Birthdays

Too many birthdays
in the orchard of guns
breakfast of idlis
from the plate of ifs
rain from the police
his highness sleeps
a fish market weeps
in the company of castes
from rotten sons
ripe dads drop down
home-made sleep
tv's recipe for war.
27.6.19

22. 21) M.G.Road

On the Mahatma Gandhi road
traffic wardens tax a further ten rupees
on a packet of table salt
At the traffic lights, auto drivers
aspire to become panchayat
presidents of foreign affairs.
At its police station, a detainee
is remanded to newspapers
To find out how he died.
Jun 2019

23. 22) Half Love

The first showers in a long summer.
Just then you arrived.
Long after I could not arrive
at the many puzzles
you threw my way.
I need to go. I am in a hurry.
Not before you take this cake and tea.
As if it was all I needed to offer you
for my final letting off.
You ate half the cake alright
And a half moon bestowed its boons
on the drowsy oleanders
meant for the morning gods.
When you left
the cup carried your shaky lip
marks . The sea's lip
marks it erases on the shores.
On the plate, sat half my love
your fingers touched.
Like an exoplanet just discovered.
Flags of love tilting at the windmills
Flutter perilously in the sea winds.
Exoplanet : a planet belonging to another star

To tilt at the windmills= To fight imaginary enemies
10.3.19.

24. 23) To meet

Fated if we are to meet again
Face-to- honest face, one day and finally,
Readied, redeemable, and in desire.
Not in a rendezvous, repressive like deep winter
Not like nightfall, stealthy and cold, wasting
Away in quanta of q-ing up qualms,
But like ..like the ocean in penance for ages
Turning blessed to pour on itself the blessings
When the ocean , past its fond madness,
Is all spring. When the air stilled unhooks
the heaving garments of light. When its
mortal hand would nimbly lift the last veil of linen,
If it is so, if we are to meet thus,
Why not even before the sun rests
Even before the sea is spring
Even as the distant geraniums wait
in readiness for another spring
in a far far away land.
21.3.19

25. 24) To part

Fated, if we are, to part
WhatsApp-weary
Or unavoidably as fate would have it
Or inescapably as they would view it.
We will go through that
Not like the earth moving away from the moon
After being in line for yet another eclipse,
Not like the tears, in union with the eyes
Thus far, finding its way out,
One day under intense grief;
But like, and more agreeably so,
How the skin-thin veil of dew would be
Ripped off the body of earth by the morning sun;
Or as the heavy star-turned-black hole
Is black with all its light
Trapped inside; or like how the love-mad
Sun would finally call it quits to lift
His sober head off the perimeter of
Earth's pelvis.
27 Mar 19

26. 25) The Lord

The army's Lord Hanuman waits
to bless two long rows of *Brahmans*,
each with a retinue of 19 gods, waiting
to witness *arati*. Census says two
of them did not eat and three cried last
night, but all have *aadhar* cards.
At the centre of the town, they hold
the annual congress of viruses.
It is now their turn to garland the
leftover uncontaminated statue.
Reservoirs are run over by used
smart phones in distant Chennai.
Further on, digital rains
do not deter China
29.6.19

27. 26) Who knocks

Who knocks at the door
Of the moon?
Fruit-eating bats or astrophysics?
Do not rock the ration shop.
Will it not collapse on to
the palace road.
Postman is on his off.
Letters on the drought type
themselves to the editor.
Listed in today's business?
Last year's cheatsheet
is still in the red.
Ten thousand books sit
on the anvil.
Wordsmith waits.
How will one find
Wordsworthian lines
On varicose veins?
Last day of June.
Calendar doubles over.
Pain in the pocket.
30.6.19

28. 27) Sleep

Sleep, deciduous sleep
sways. Lightly sheds,
in the dark, printer's black,
hard-disk-saved night.
And now,
a love-leaf drops
trance-trills awhile
soaks in the deep-touched
seepage from the sky…
sleeps in the dawn's dew-hug.
A wrath-leaf drops,
wabbit-wiggles about
until the gasp blows
it stars-away.
Finally the sleep-leaf falls
goes deep into sleep
sleep into night
night into day.
3.7.19

29. 28) Channel 5

The two sit watching
He from her chair and she from his knees
Barbara Windsor story on air
'You have made me a lady', Barbara
exclaims and lounges forward
at her man staring in disbelief.
She starts giggling and it won't stop
'You have made me a man'
He whispers in her ear
Promptly, she slides down
to the carpeted floor;
and her robes too.
A naïve duvet thinks it keeps away
The leftover cold of the Mayfair air.
Feb 19

30. 29) Begone despair

Begone despair, leave him alone,
Go pick on someone else; some one
From another staging post,
To impose your amorphous writ.
Begone woes, leave him alone,
In this world of redacted selves.
Him with a shambolic mien
Bestowed by a revanchist vein.
Begone pain, leave him alone,
Him with heart and limb in pain,
Him that moans and winces all day,
Him in a glib and flippant world.
Feb 2019.

31. 30) A valentine one

I know you now crave for me,
Like an empty Jar, its honey.
Remember, you are in me,
Like how , in Vishnu, was Lakshmi
When treasured by the milk-sea.
Feb 2019

Note: Goddess Lakshmi emerged from the sea of milk when it was churned by gods and demons. Lord Vishnu however received her as his consort.

32. 31) Conflict

Conflict is creative, they wisely declare;
but is it not conflagration too?
Or even a fusion bomb.
Losers all, screwing up, with words come easy,
oblique, hazy. Poor beings who need
a romance running to even scribble
a condolence note.
Alas, devils meant to delve into words
putting strictures on them.
With them anything goes.
Consoling is condescending.
Meaning is demeaning.
Put them in chains, the crackpots.
Listen to Plato. Banish them all
from the republic.
For shanti, for peace.
Six year olds playing house ever at six,
runny-nosed, snuffly, grumpy.
Now cheery, now butting heads.
Forgive them. Om shanti.
Mandukya:
Om iti etad aksharam idam sarvam.
(Om is ALL)

ALL, LL, L.
(L like in Love, not like in loss)
Om iti etad aksharam udgeetham upaseeta
(Meditate on Om as udgeeta)
Udgeeta, dgeeta, geeta, eeta,
eta, ta, a.
(a like the u in but, not butt)
Feb 19

33. 32) Thames

For a moment I sat tasting the Bru
My tv made and unmade.
Their flavoured offer to the coffee-world.
When I overheard little children breaking
The news of the day; that of the toy car
One of them gave her friend as a b day gift,
And how Amy did not know how to work it.
But, your verses from the past seem
to have lost none of its past and present.
Which once found me flying into your febrile nest.
You haven't written a line since.
Where did it all go. Did it leave you the moment
I came in, even as men with wooden wives
walked the high street, taking in
the tang of the Thames air.

34. 33) Post mod artists

Is spitting me out
Like an apple pip
As chic as
Stealing off me a greedy bite?
Or not letting your lip
Sync with the sip
As easy,
If I am your coffee, right?
You ardent post-mod artists
Avid eaters of burnt parts
Are unburnt parts
Meant to be cast away?
10 Mar 19.

35. 35) Kuchipudi

Through her performance, I sat
discovering you, fragment by fragment,
through a sequence of nimble misses;
misses that were not there in her
butterfly feet, mudras, and the music that rose
and fell at her feet and discovered itself.
Till I discovered you in full in the glint
of her eyes as it missed out on Krishna's love,
and her voice in his invisible flute.
Of course, it was tough finding you.
Even the Manipuri that followed
struggled for an hour to find itself.
Feb 19

36. 34) Love poem

I write a post modern love poem
On a sheet of mineral water.
From the time dawn had its dawnness
I did not think. I never reasoned.
I found even the TV got its share of love from me.
No news however good sizzled
and no news however bad fizzled, when it broke.
The grammatically minded ones may
Replace news with love and it with heart.
Even the shut-down that did not
happen yet had possibilities open.
Though the conspiracy constantly
parried the stock question.
The rationally minded may also believe
the statement in its future tense.
And outside, the rains or shut downs
or whatever stopped the trains.
Nature enters the discourse
because love is to the living
what milk is to Milma
or water is to milk.
Seniors, untired of deluges
Killed themselves in and out of it.

I might join in.
Let her not know.
Jan 19

37. 36) Fractions

Now, of fractions. That was before
we quarreled on quotients.
That was even before we compromised
on compositions of history.
Before that it was economics, echoes
of money. But that was fractious.
That was how we remembered
The math and history of fractions.
Feb 19

38. 37) Sonnet

How do we handle a past that hurts.
The questions about our worst moments,
the whirlpools of memory,
the rapids of reflection. A memory that
should be more beautiful than another woman,
more peaceable than another sunset in the ocean.
And at last an uneasy sunrise.
The difference between life and death.
There is no distance between us.
Can't we find one word, in place of two, to describe us.
The word that would keep our rift apart.
Let us fit in a 14th line to make it a modern sonnet.
Mar 19

39. 38) Hu R U

You give me my wings, when I soar in the sky.
To the stars of my sky, you give them their winks.
And to those starry winks, their timeless light years,
And to the light years, more than their lights.
And when down I come, you yield to my desire,
Just as swiftly as it takes to say 'I love you'.
Just as simple as that. Who indeed are you?
Jan 19

40. 39) Hu R U 2

Into the heavens I go, at the thought of you.
Day or night, rain or shine, vales or Wales;
And coast down those heady heights
Canoodling like mad, your delicate frame,
All aflutter. And strangely, down here
On this mortal dirt, home or hotel, road or car,
Alone together with all the darkness for cover
I would not so much as touch you.
And, would sit with the self-control,
A seer would be proud of.
Who indeed are you.
In which bygone age did we meet first?

41. 40) Artesian

It was the sudden opening up
Of an artesian well.
Even as it grew less copious,
It yielded me bucketfuls.
It had gone dry since.
So, I drill deep to find its springs.
For, I have in my lips its taste
The taste a baby has for titmilk.
But how was it that it was,
Of all the persons, your love?
7.3.19

42. 41) Blossoms

As our feeble winter wore out,
The mango tree went 'blooms',
With its painted dome of panicles
And its softie scent wafting in.
I dreamt of sacks full of mangoes.
Then, after a night of gentle drizzles
Though tender like a shower of dew
I woke up to a tree shorn of its promise
Standing in a bed of fallen dreams.
How was it that your love
Turned out to be those blossoms?
7.3.19
42) Shooting Star
The sky-gazer that I was
Was bored with a deadpan sky,
When a shining light streaking through
Lit up the sky and lifted my heart.
Who knew it was a shooting star
Who knew it was you ?.
7.3.19.

43. 42) Shooting star

The sky-gazer that I was
Was bored with a deadpan sky,
When a shining light streaking through
Lit up the sky and lifted my heart.
Who knew it was a shooting star
Who knew it was you ?.
7.3.19.

44. 43) POW

When your Mirage pretty
Crossed the line of control
Flew into my air
I rose in the sky and we
Faced each other.
True to your name
Back and forth chasing
Manoeuvres many
Missiling each other down
Both of us ejected
Both landed on your land
Though hurt, free you are
But, thrown to torture
I am your prisoner of war.
Who would believe
Ours was more war
Than stuff of lore.
15.3.19

45. 44) Keys Again

I lose keys, all the time, travelling.
Here, they don't seem to have bolt-cutters,
like they do, over there.
The day I landed at the airport
and lost my suitcase key
your dad drove down with one
to break that little lock in two.
His hearty smile, naughty wink,
as he made his way out.
That, by the way,
was our only sacrament
and rite of passage.
Here, in hotels they come
with terrible-looking tools, and fail
to break the back of my poor
locks, my conscience keepers.
This time, they went electric.
Swish…it's over in a second.
Sign of progress .
So, consciences are easy to kill these days.
That must be global warming.
Jan 19

46. 45) XMAS

Christmas I missed and Easter too
But not the Christmas feast, that too in May
Up against all else
Up in the hilltop house
Turkey roast, potatoes boiled, potatoes roast
Broccoli, carrots, and parsnips
Asparagus and green beans
And to break it, the special cranberry sauce
Complete with gravy
Minus of course the cabbage in cheese
Cheese, anyway, I was cheesed off with.
Wait for the round of the town
Promised to Faith.
2. 4. 19

47. 46) Blind post

To meet on a blind post, so to say,
And to greet in metaphors
More in the make than in the break
We who never did know
Let alone size up each other,
But, were too sure of the who
Who was who but who.
And thus here we are
Finger tips on keypads
Prodded by keyed up fads
To meet, for all we wish,
Eye to pleasing eye, ear to willing ear,
Word to meaningful word
Surrender to soulful surrender
Sunday through Saturday
Yet, slippery a way
Hopefully not for another hurt
But for another heart
Not the selfsame selfie maker
From the past.
13 Apr 19

48. 47) Tea break

At last, we took
a tea-break in silence
in the time of love; the silence
that you said would
sink into our hearts.
But you drew out a little caution
to gently dissuade me from my
habit of bingeing on sweets.
But, then, we were at
a way side eatery.
So, we will
have tea at home next time
that too brewed by you,
when we will
take turns taking sips
of silence
from the same cup.
16 Apr 2019

49. 48) Strokes

Those days I have
Oftentimes stroked you to sleep.
And, every time you so slept,
you said, you dreamt of a sun
stroking the fire with a broom.
But, every time
I rather irreverently joked:
Different strokes for different folks.
Just to enjoy your discomfiture
Or was it a leg-upped prettiness.
After many years
when the sun is setting
on me, I too need strokes,
of a different kind,
to my aching joints.
Which makes you joke: Yes, indeed.
Different strokes to different aches
One's own strokes to one's own aches.
18 Apr 19

50. 49) The Wheelchair

Corridors snaky across exclusive blocks
Not often you get a wheelchair to navigate them.
But a limp in your walk will do the trick.
They would put you in one and push you around.
But, there is no sure limp in life's testing corridors
And proving grounds, that would put you
In a wheelchair, while others take over the pushing.
Feb 19.

51. 50) Shutdown

Since you were not happy
With life's traditional provocations.
I gave you hartal to try.
A welcome void on our civic
and civilisational ruins called roads.
Asked where, I pointed you to
The open fields of demo-crazy
And its first cousins,
Playing barefoot in their shorts.
Asked how, I showed you the stones
Which your primitive forefathers
Used to kill for meat,
Which you can now use to kill
For booze, parottas, and beef.
Jan 19

52. 51) Twelfth man

One, two, three
Up the brittle tree
Ego for free.
No great guy
No one to buy
Standing by
Four five six
Net gets its fix
Attitudinizing mix
Bat and ball on
Rolls on the lawn
If, hurt, lies John
Ten eleven
Like leaven
Unholy heaven
Indefinite wait
For a kindly fate
& an innings great.
Note: on the line= at risk
10.6.19

53. 52) Rain

It was as the rains
That you came in, this day,
Falling slowly and steadily
Showering kisses upon the earth.
But, the sniffle you gave me last time
Had not gone away yet,
So I don't wet myself this time
But watch you from the balcony
And catch a few drops of your love
In my cupped palms
Which I continue to hold
In remembrance of my love;
After you went away suddenly.
You know how painful it is
To stand that way
Till my sniffle goes away
And you fall again
From your golden heavens.
14.6.19

54. 53) Love-wet

Can't forget you yet
Rain on the roses
Love-wet gift.
Jun 19

55. 54. Slowguns

In a land where kids go dead
On the morn after they went to bed
With nothing to eat
Save the litchi fruit
In a land where the docs
Blame it on the heat wave
When a shot of dextrose
Would have saved the day
In this land of slogans
Of every damn kind
That promises the moon
If I lie dead
And you find me cry
It will be only for you.
16.6.19

56. 55. For You

For the sweet-toothed me, you-know-what.
For the you-know-what, the time
For time, the full moon
For the moon, love
For love, you
For you
Who (ooo)
Hi (iii)
10.7.19

57. 56. Gift

Your soul-sourced gift sits by The Gita's
Self-set directive, as a bookmark in it;
A strip of cardboard scrawled over with
Your weep-seep word.
For, my silver chest has little space.
For, in there, for you, my love-ruby bursts.
11.7.19

58. 57. Uphill

Last time, we made it half way up
This lofty height, hand in hand,
Looking for the high
of the sky meeting its lunar night.
Midway through, something broke
And the planned rendezvous went for a toss.
The river below skirting it
in a loose dialogue began to speak
in an alien tongue.
Today, I trudge up the hill, alone.
There is no you.
But, even this day, my love-weary
feet, wherever they touch, should give
the earth goosebumps,
but, its laughter just slaughters
every hill around where love lives on.
I would make it to where
the clouds put a finger on
the quivering lips of the hearts' will.
The carefree river now in a sleep-walk
has a new night every hour
as it layers them up to make a day.
14.7.19

59. 58. Chandrayaan-2

58) Chandrayaan-2

At the end of the day, like in love, it is not the gravity-defying speed that matters, but how the lander and rover softland, be it on rock or in a crater.

That the lark in the park found on the way did not sing was but an omen missed. But, if it was thinking up its swan song, it was unlike a lark.

Sunflowers do not bloom on moon. There are no moonflowers either, because they just don't exist, though water-lilies lay quiet in water parks.

Looking for moondirt and stardust when you do not yet know how to make roads that last their first season of rains.

Thank god, no one had ever reported landslides on moon. Nor a tsunami in case it held a smileless ocean in its heart. But that was how things worked out.

We rubbed hands to warm up the hearts that froze, and shook hands to suppress the hackles that rose. Not a sub-zero status of faults yet.

Whether it was close to the flowchart or not, we failed to rewrite the script. The half inch margin stands out in clarity, though, for whoever wants to scribble their new scripts on.

Sept 19.

60. 59) River

The rains stopped, even as the sky was not clear yet. That was when I tried to row her across the river. The river had no end, but too many bends into minds. It had length, length that went into the heart.

Winding and winding it but went
Into where the oar sent
It into the night. The oar carried
The day. My mind wore out the night.

I did not know hunger because I was myself hunger that only the butterflies knew. The hunger that stroked her hair and braided them into plaits of memory.

Still, all was either rain or water.
The water that swelled up like the sea.
The sea was but her tresses
That swept over the bum of mystery.

Our limbs were roses that refused to wilt in the sun. And, at sea we unmade love and offered it to our gods. Something like the last rites. Of impracticably pious souls. Fully fed, the spirits enquire piously. Where at all did you meet up. In the rowboat or in the river?

Where indeed did we?
But, what a question when she is
already a small ocean in my eyes.

Oct 2, 19.

61. 60) Day

The day sought its nook in the autorickshawcracy-afflicted city, finding ways amidst its tsunami of scooters. Like a worm on a blade of grass, pulp from the pounding of rains, that holds its own at its tip for a moment before latching on to the next.

It tasted blood from the hotel kitchens where beef mingled with Bengali sweat, and sought comfort zones in the sweaty armpits of confused housewives.

It could not take in more. Like their disdains or the city's teasing math. Or reverie in the stink of the working class upon the scent of socialist glint, or seek solace in the sips of the black labeled bitch.

The time instead relaxes by the tea stall with a cup of the bare black in hand. Under the tree of noisy crows that go silent when they shit into your cup.

Oct 19.

62. 61) Early morning meditation

Cleave the night,
roll up sleep, sit,
collect the light;
The loveful light,
love that could be
misspelt as lowe, or
a lo-we hyphenate…
A door opens.
The sound of water
and toothbrush
whispering away
fatigue and bad breath.
Light again…The tea
you crave which is just
a t mixed with an ea,
two bodies hinged
in habit. Light now off
turns on again…
Front door opens. And
a stressed world out there
like the first sloppy draft
of a write you posted

in haste. And it is again
light, until it is not.

Note: The interruptions to meditation in which you concentrate on a light that is full of love deep inside the heart.

10 oct 19

63. 62) Kanyakumari

When my death dies on a fifth,
you will have dropped down
To the bottom fifth of my chat list that
Starts with an Either and ends with an Or.
That would be a sunny day,
You realize that, whether it is meteorology,
or parrot-astrology, there is no
foretelling of rains in one's life.
Rains within five days or five weeks
Or five months, the parrot man said.
Not five years ?, I queried.
He did not like it.
Days that are teases, mangy, slimy
Oozing from between tongue and treason.
They lay suspended between
The photo man's grin and
The peanut boy's nape,
Bypassed his pidgin Hindi
Of its slim-butted beach,
Of Mayiamma's no-speech
Across the Chicago rock
And the pinnacle of pious sermons
And dipped into half memories

Where I once stood as a boy
Immersing my mother's ashes
Long before global warming
And liberal democracy
Set, for the tri-sea its tolerance limits.
The last fifth of the ashes meant for
The waters, the water on which the massive
Suchindram chariot is set to float one day *
With possibly a bait dangling beneath it
To catch a future life form
After the final floods.
'Tvam Brahma, tvam yajna, tvam loka:
*Aham Brahma, aham yajna, aham loka:'***
That is when all the logy's and logic
Would cohere in life to hit the last fifth
Of death, after its four-fifths have
Already been eaten up by life's crushes
And curses upping and dipping
Like ever new apps.
Oct 2019

Note:

*Akilatirattu, the sacred book of a local sect is said to predict that the world ends after three days of deluge, when the flood waters would carry the chariot(Which should weigh a few tons) of the Sucheendram temple to the sea at Kanyakumari some fifteen kms away.

**A father about to die is supposed to perform the following rite of passage, transferring his responsibilities to the son :
Father says: You are the supreme Lord, you are the sacrifice, you are the world.
The son replies : I am the supreme Lord, I am the sacrifice, I am the world.
(Brihadaranyaka Upanishad)

64. 63) Elections

1
Giving each other
runs for their monies
are the LCM and the HCF.
2
Promises flow.
Water in Thar, Smiles in Tihar.
Smiles Tihar
3
Votes travelled north
where EVM's are magic
4
Voters travelled south where
borewells swallow two year olds.
5
Electronics takes over elections.
Electionics damns electronics.
6
Sun or rain bath to the home sick,
home bound. Insanes just laugh.
7
Consti(pated)tuencies awaiting
results to have the runs.

Oct 2019

65. 64. Pain

The light, the dark, the waters,
the air, the snigger, the hurt.
I was all that.
The birds, the mornings, the blooms,
the smiles, the routine orange alerts.
You were all that.
They are not us anymore,
the new alphabet, math, history.
The Sorry Memorial School curriculum.
'You have the refuge of love.
Is this not a precious gift?'
Asks the morning's whatsApp post.
They think we are duds.
This is not cinema. Not love either,
the kind of phlegm the hollow poet
coughs up and calls love.
It is just pain beyond
all Pallium-Indias, that grows from
the roots, the fruits and the shoots.
Pain, bar coded and packed that won't
sell itself short. After all these
offputting miles. Is there some law
at least against the miles?

Nov 2019.

66. 65. Misstakes

'Let us make better mistakes tomorrow'
Tomorrow? Forget today?
Forget the rice left to boil on the stove?
Leave it for tomorrow?
Mistakes? Heap them.
Better upon better.
Misstakes with an extra yes
that makes them better.
That makes it cooked.
Nov 2019.

67. 66. Unliveable

Against a large pall of doubts
the morning sun hangs loose
by its burning stubble of hydrogen.
The suicide squad of scooterists
are out on the roads' ruins
left over by the Panipet wars.
To be soon joined by the auto
and car bandits prowling
the roads' Chambal ravines.
Life is more sweetly unliveable,
though; c/o the stiff office babus,
sundry softwares, and cyanides.
Life is hot, molten, killed and lived
under the comfy folds
of a cushioned something.
Like in love, so blended and bonded
that, though bloodied and in
sleep mode, it is not curtains yet.
Nov 2019

68. 67. You

The pretty little line of poetry
that pops up in me suddenly
before it vanishes in a flash,
and is now my despair, as I can't
retrieve it, however much I try;
That is you.
Even as I find no time for whatever
I need to do, when time
finds me to find you;
Then time is you.
When reminded by Einstein
that time is a stubborn illusion,
and there is nothing like
a present, past, or future;
The timeless is you.
All that my poetry sings of
and all that it does not
and all that it will;
All that is you.
Even as I don't want to pen
another line, the poetry that
erupts all over me like measles
and wont let me sleep;

That again is you.
All those zero's and one's that
stream through the fine fibres,
antennas and empty spaces of my being;
All that is digital you.
The supernova that bursts in my mind
and the pulsar whose beams sweep
over me every five minutes;
Both are you.
And finally, when the Milky Way
and the Andromeda catch up
with each other to merge
into one, in a billion years;
It will once again be you.
Nov 2019

69. 68. Ignorance is Bliss

Ignorance was not blings, when the earth
was not round. Remember Galileo.
When it had come round to being round,
poly-ticks sat between anx and ings.
A yummy elliptical pie, with Galileo long gone.
Ings became a delicious mix of cream and kingdoms.
Alas, altitudes spurt out of craters and clay pots
like cream from critters. Orated up by
the soap box wizards of the new fangled
Townships caught in the crosswires
of jack fruit and traffic jams.
Call them the savior-of-all types.
Remember mating dogs.
Pleasure in the pelvis. Pain in the penis.
The hugs and kisses between will and weakness.
Between storm drains and rat piss.
Not easy piss offs, them, though.
Need to flood and floodlight the drains
Until then it is heights and distances.
15-11-2019

70. 69. God

From the midst of the savage race
of a savage race on the roads,
all that gets you back home
in one piece is god's grace.
Traffic rules are just helmets and hefty fines.
From the treacherous doings
Meant for breaking bonds,
what keeps you sane is god's blessings.
Friendship is just brittle glass.
Remember the cyanide
Remember the wronged artist
Remember the mangled genitals
Remember the daily dead
The morning's papers do.
'Aum, remember the deeds remember,
Remember the deeds, remember'.
Whether it is planning commission
Or Niti Ayog,
Please make plans to find
The humanity in man that he lost
Since he found Freedom.

71. 70. Closing the Divide

Rogue rains in the carnival times
Cholera in the times of romance
Nettles did Suryanamaskar to a no-sun
A lone scooterist asked the muddied
sheet of water for directions
.
Mad midnight raps on the rooftops.
Doors connected to the spillgates of the hills
Waters broke like in a miscarriage of sorts.
Water is life (scripture-style)
Life in water (media-style)
Our ROM's read help as rowboat;
Need as packed food, bottled water and pads;
Smile as sun and warmth, minus slime,
Detritus, water snake and leech.
Constituencies fused. Conscience rose.
The world wore the ready-to-do-good gear.
Applause from far and near.
Sun got up. Apocalypse in retreat.
Conscience shut down.
Fault lines reappeared.
No 70court said no to the shutdown yet.
Who said yes?

Dec 2019

Note: A flood poem

72. 71. Missile

The digital missile of feelings shot across
the sky will be in flight, in silent mode,
before it would find you; the beaming
star, the gleaming moon or whatever;
and when it does catch up with you
in a pigeon hole that would just suffice
to sheath your nakedness, stripped
as you are of fire, power, powder
and your branded attire; having dumped
your skin in language, having outgrown
your mind into how the sun would one day
outgrow itself into discarding this world.
Dec 2019

9 798887 728247

Printed by Libri Plureos GmbH in Hamburg, Germany